Moments of Grace

by

Melissa Cooper

Strategic Book Publishing
New York, NewYork

Strategic Book Publishing
An imprint of AEG Publishing Group
845 Third Avenue, 6th Floor - 6016
New York, NY 10022
www.StrategicBookPublishing.com

ISBN: 978-1-60693-835-5
SKU: 1-60693-835-5

Printed in the United States of America

Book Design: Rolando F. Santos

Contents

Dedicated with a Gracious Heart
to
My Beloved Branden

The Journey

Me, Myself, and God

I SIT within myself and wonder what it is like to be truly alone. My soul has opened to learn my own truth, and there is a numbness that surrounds my heart. I'm scared of feeling my emptiness, I fear what I may see, yet I move through the walls of all my existence like a warrior princess fighting for her freedom. I have traveled through the mountainous terrain, unlocked the chains that have left me hanging, floated down turbulent rivers, and battled with my enemies, knowing that I am not fighting for my life. I am fighting for love—a love so embedded within my soul that it hurts. My heart aches, longing and searching for this connection. I am so scared of being in the physical world, loving a God from whom I can feel so isolated. Yet, in all this, my heart remains full of love.

Is this it? I cry out. Is this my only purpose here: to love you?

YES!

Where is the greatness in loving you? I ask of God.

In the moment, you realize love is your only gift of survival. It can never be taken from you; you must give of love first. It will never die with you because it is the life force that continues long after your physical being has gone. It never leaves you because your soul will perish without love. Even though you may exist, how will you immerse yourself in the beauty and drama of life if you cannot feel love?

How can you truly live if you have not love?

Love all things, even the indifference of all life. Give of yourself until your heart bleeds from the sheer joy of giving love. Give every tear of hope, every pain, and every suffering until you find peace in your soul and until loving what is becomes a way of life. Love me, believe in me, and you will see the truth of who you really are: that which is love. Where else would you rather be?

Beautiful Love

Breathe in; drink from your radiance. Breathe out; let go
     of all that is repressed.
I touch the essence of my soul through my heart.
I am loved by God. Briefly, I see the world through your
     eyes.
I am open to receive, yet fearful of what this means.
I have peace within the knowing, and my heart is
     warmed with your guidance that all is perfect and
     where it needs to be.
Trust in me, you say.
Let go and let God, you say.
I am waiting for you. Are you ready to receive me, you
     say.
Why is this love so deep that to pierce the heart creates
     the pain I desire
and increases my need to be close to you, yet I still run
     the other way.
This love is so beautiful that to embrace it,
to allow grace to find a home in my soul, to love you and
     be loved by you,
I would have to love myself. . . .
Beautiful, beautiful, beautiful love.

Merciful Heart

There is such a divine light that shines from your eyes,
and through this vision of grace,
I am moved to be humbled by
my merciful heart.
It is in the forgiveness of self that I have laid to rest my
        pain,
allowed the peaceful being to emerge whole
and completely in love with God,
my merciful heart.
I have surrendered into this vast ocean of consciousness,
and in this house of gratitude,
my soul connects with all I have longed for,
my merciful heart.
With the tears I cry
as I ache to lie joyfully in this heavenly place,
I have prayed for this love as
I graciously give to
my merciful heart.
You are the breath in all that surrounds me.
You are my eternal existence each time I awake to a new
        day.
I know you will rest in love forever.
God bless my merciful heart.

God of Love

As I lie surrendered, I give to the God of love,
my heart overflows like a river to the ocean.
In this moment, I am everything, yet nothing. I am free.
 My union is made whole, and my true essence radiates
        unconditional, pure,
and beautiful love.
I am grounded in the knowing that when the ocean of
        love is rough,
I will swim in these waters peacefully and play with
        Thee.
It is my love of God, sailing through an endless sea, that
        rests in my heart of serenity. . . .
God bless.

Surrender

My heart aches for that which I have not touched today.
My soul is guiding me, but I cannot hear the words it is
      saying.
I am clouded in this longing for love within myself,
but it is You I crave.
As we meet, I hunger for the intimacy I have shared.
My chest lay open and my heart revealed
as I give completely to this love.
I taste you, I touch you, and now I have seen you.
I cry in ecstasy as I surrender into you.
Then I realize that, in this moment,
I have been loved by God.

The Wisdom of the Soul

Heartfelt Moments.

Let love flow through you,
and you start living.

Make love a celebration,
and your life will become an unforgettable experience.

The moment you accept yourself,
you become beautiful.

Experience a miracle, look closely at yourself,
and you will see the greatest miracle of all.

The wings of your consciousness unfold, your cocoon
unravels, and your soul has finally opened to love.
Even a caterpillar has extraordinary beauty,
which evolves into the most beautiful butterfly: YOU!

The language of silence is the language of love. This is God
speaking softly to your heart.

Return to love, find your joy,
transcend your journey into a way of acceptance,
and you will come home to the divine.

Trust in the journey of life
and know that the outcome you seek awaits.
Let this ignite your passion and awaken your senses....
Your life is exciting.

Flow with life, be with life,
live your life without boundaries.
This will not define you; this will set you free.

Don't live a repressed life; otherwise, you live not at all.
Live a life of expression, creativity, and joy.

There is a sequence that leads from one to another:
a way of love, natural and inevitable.

Every opportunity lost
is an expression of your soul missed.

You are a gift from God; honor all that you are.
You are magnificent; it's your time to shine.

The way of enlightenment is the way of a peaceful heart.
It is where you are right now.

Stop searching for God.
God is before you. Open your eyes from blindness, and
only then will you exist.

Flow into your body, and you will flow into life.
Listen to your body, and you will find
the answer you have being searching for.

Come alive with the Holy Spirit;
feel its warmth move through you,
every cell of your body and your mind.
Open your heart, and you begin to accept
the help that God is offering.

Accept whatsoever you are.
You are a great mystery of many energies.
Move with your energy, with a deep sensitivity.
Flow with awareness, with love, with understanding.
Then every desire becomes a vehicle to go beyond.
Every energy becomes your guide.
Your world becomes divine. Your body is your temple,
a holy place, your holy place for God's grace. . . .

Stop struggling. Allow the flow of grace,
and still your beating heart.
Honor the cycle of consciousness.
Your butterfly is emerging, and soon she will take flight,
hold hands with God, and be free.

There are moments in your life
that will move through you like the ebb of the ocean,
in and out with the tides.
Stop arguing with yourself. All is perfect; all is divine.
It is a timeless wait, then divinity arrives,
the yearning subsides, and you have peace.

Be humbled by your life experiences and know that all
the imperfections you have been shown are perfect.
This is love knocking at the door to your heart.
She will guide you and be your shining light,
leading the way home.

Every day that I honor my body,
I am accepting the wonderful temple
that is home to my mind and soul, allowing me to radiate love,
showing me how beautiful I truly am,
opening my heart to the magic of life.

Your heart is an open channel,
moving naturally with the flow of life.
Complete in the circle of evolution,
yet physically this life is not finished
for this magnificent child of God.
Being is part of the existence;
existing becomes a way of being.
Then, without warning,
a new journey erupts like fireworks.
Joy fills the body like bubbles,
overflowing as the elixir of life becomes blissful,
and for a moment you remember how to live!

Not a day goes by that I am not eternally grateful for.
Everything is perfect and where it needs to be. As it is in
heaven, so it is on earth.
You are perfect just where you are right now; there is no need
for change....

Be still, listen, and you will hear
the serenade that your soul is singing.

There is no greater love
than the choice to love others as they are.
In that love your heart is unlocked,
and you are free to love yourself.
Divine and beautiful all you need to do is use the key,
unlock the door, have a peek, and see the real you....

Have faith, trust, believe, and—above all these—know
that I am by your side and your prayers are answered
at that moment. Allow my grace to flow through you
and stop arguing with the logic of the mind, for in the
universe of all things, all things are possible. Step aside
and allow my love for you to shine the star of hope and
give you the miracle you have asked for.

Open your soul to be a channel of grace,
and the presence of God will emanate from your heart
and be the inspiration for others who journey
on their own inner path to God.

A new dawn, a new day, a new earth,
and a new way of being.
Let go of all fear, and immerse yourself
in a fragrant bath of love.
Drown yourself, and you will be reborn
into a love so precious.
The light that shines from your soul
is the reflection of God smiling at you.

14   *Melissa Cooper*

I am completely in awe of my existence.
Every day is a miracle.
Every breath I take is a moment created in life
when magic happens, and I am rendered speechless.

God is all things, and in all things,
the seeker shall find God.

Love, happiness, courage, peace, harmony, and forgiveness.
These are the six precepts of life. Live them, feel them, and
when you feel like running from them,
don't bother. They will find you.

When I close my eyes,
I am transported into the soul of all life.
The Magic of God's beauty surrounds me.
I am healed from blindness.
Every breath I take is a cherished moment.
Every step I take is a miracle.

Thank You.

The Heart of My Beloved

The Heart of My Beloved

There are moments in our lives you will remember.
This is one moment like that: our connection,
our souls dancing gracefully to reconnect to this love.
My brother, my sister, my mother, my father, my Creator.
    There is nothing for which we are separate in this
    beautiful place we have come to share.
Though we are unconscious to the greater vision and
    purpose of our lives,
we surrender into and trust this untravelled road we
    walk upon
in the hope that we can reconnect with our souls.
And in these silent prayers to God, we start each day
    as if it were our last. Embrace love and cherish all
    who cross our path as we connect to these moments
    with a fragile heart.
It is the human spirit to wonder and to create the stories
    in our lives we wish to play out. In the drama of
    our hearts' desires, the peace and freedom from our
    own suffering is flowering in the Valley of Eden,
    which we can share with our beloved friends.
I know in my own awareness that you are a beloved
    friend, and for every thought I have of you, I will
    pick a wild flower from the Valley of Eden and
    offer this token of gratitude to God for the blessing
    that is you.

Thank You

I am in awe of your beauty as a man with whom I long to
        share my
body, mind, and soul.
I am touched by your gracious embrace,
and I am humbled by the experience of loving you.

Beloved

Beloved,
like the vast oceans that flow deeply into the portals of
    life,
so you are that ocean in mine.
You are the embodiment of God,
and as we meet in this house of love, I touch what I have
    longed for…

Beloved,
it is your soul that permeates every cell of my being
and breathes new life into my heart
as I rest in gratitude for all that you are to me…

Beloved,
I am but a lotus flower always in bloom,
and you water and nurture this flower
so that one day it may give its beauty in the sweet scent
    of your garden.

Beloved,
I have seen the true essence of your being radiating the
    purest light of gold.
Your love is lightened with each breath of God, ever-
    changing like
Maya, Shanti, Shiva, Shakti.
Moving closer to the truest spirit of self, you are not
    merely just a man;
you are the divinity of that which a man can be,
in the likeness of God.

Beloved,
I am blessed to love you and drink from the radiance you
    propel into my life.
I am humbled by your words of love
as you open the door for me to move closer to
    consciousness.
I am made whole and become the essence of woman and
    goddess in sharing this with you.

Beloved,
I don't need you to feel complete, but my soul longs to
    connect with your soul.
I am not consumed by desire, yet I immerse myself in the
    passion of each moment.
I love you not for what you can give me, but for what
    you share with me
in the deepest recesses of your body and your mind.
I am not waiting nor yearning for you, but I will
    surrender to you in love completely.

Beloved,
as I look into your eyes, I see the vast ocean that we both
    sail in together.
I know that each portal we reach in life will be blessed by
    God.
And although at times these blessings are confronting
    and delicate, they bring us both closer
to a union of truth within ourselves and each other.

Beloved,
there is nothing for us to be except that which we already
    are.
For, in each moment we share, everything our
    relationship can be is already there.
I pray that this union moves with the flow of love in
    intimacy and consciousness, blossoming into the
    Garden of Eden where we can both live.

Beloved,
you inspire me and remind me that this dance of love I
        perform in life is to awaken my soul
to the beauty it can truly share with everyone and be the
        essence of what I long for.

Beloved,
I give to you without condition, and I embrace you with
        complete acceptance
of the magnificent being you emanate to me.
 I pray that you always know God and be inspired by
        your own passions to dance
your dance of love
and give of your radiance, opening doors for others to
        realize their truth.
I love you with each breath of God.

Honoring You

I celebrate my love for you today, as our hearts open and
      we surrender into this magic.
We have completed the circle of life, and our souls have
      found their way home;
we have moved into the light.
My heart is soft, and my body is warm as I give in to the
      beauty of us.
We are lovers of the divine.
The road we have travelled on, none less greater than the
      other, through fear, pain, and loneliness to embrace
      each other.
I have honored you many lives before, but none as I do
      now.
You are the beauty that surrounds my world; you are the
      peace within my soul. God has graciously blessed
      our lives to make our union whole.
Our hearts are alive, and today I am humbled by the love
      I feel for you.

The Union

My compassionate heart knows no boundaries;
my soul is transcending all that I knew of love.
I am resting in silence, a blissful knowing that I have
    obtained peace.
My soul has become a union of divine love—
a love so painful it is the sheer ecstasy of loving all that
    is.
Joy emanates from every cell of my being, immersing
    myself in an ocean of light.
The flower is in bloom, sharing of its nectar to all that
    taste, touch,
 and smell its sweetness.
A love unconditional, your soul will long to connect.
You come back to this flowering pond, aware that with a
    humble heart
you are opening your inner beauty and acknowledging
    your own divinity,
your beloved, your God.

An Everlasting Moment

Your soul ignites the fire in mine,
and as I look into the blue of the ocean,
I am mesmerized by the passion I see in your eyes.
A beautiful man stands before me,
yet there is a vulnerability in his heart.
I see your strength and determination for what you
      believe,
yet you melt into an eternal being of love every time we
      kiss.
I see your courage and the silence of not speaking your
      truth,
yet when you surrender into the ecstasy of unconditional
      love, it all falls away.
I see your pain that rests in the cup of your heart,
yet when our bodies merge as one,
your cup overflows; all your pain disappears.
Every moment shared is truly a beautiful manifestation
      of what we both long for.
If I could take your suffering and pain to give you an
      everlasting moment of love,
I would graciously share this with you.

The Gift of Joy

My inspiration, my muse,
I open up my heart full of grace and gratitude
for the love you give.
I am humbled and blessed with this experience of loving
        you.
I have been given a gift: the gift of joy.
And in the vision of love when I lose myself in your eyes,
I see eternity. I see unity.
I see the oneness of you and me.

Just for You

Every moment we share together is precious and
        beautiful.
The mere thought of you ignites the passion within me,
arousing my senses that awaken my soul.
I know we will dance this dance of love together for
        eternity,
no matter the journey we share,
and my heart will rest peacefully knowing that our souls
        have joined as one.

As I look into your eyes, I see myself engaged in love
        with you;
I am made whole and complete;
and the essence of true love
emanates from every cell of my body.
I am humbled by gratitude that you have come into my
        life
so that we may share unconditional, divine love.

You are magnificent ,
and I am blessed, that you have opened your heart to me.
You are a beautiful reflection of the world that surrounds
        me,
as my heart longs to connect and my body aches to
        merge with you.
This beautiful, sacred space that we create together
will allow us to surrender in to a true blessing of love
        that is ours to share.

My Aphrodisiac

My aphrodisiac, my elixir.
My senses have awakened to a knowing of love,
a middle path of existence where the heightened state of
      being connects to the physical, where heaven and
      earth meet.
My soul is alive with the magic of what we create.
We have transcended the need for sex and opened our
      bodies and minds to the true essence
of sensuality, an erotic metamorphosis where desire and
      passion merge energies and become one.
This is ecstasy; this is utopian bliss; this is an ocean of
      unconditional love.
The orgasm of me within you and you within me,
where all we need do is breathe.

Inner Sanctum

Freedom

I have emerged from the safety of my cocoon, and I
feel so removed from within myself. My cellular body
remembers life as it was, and my ego grieves for who
she used to be. I look at myself and the perception is
beautiful, yet somehow I don't feel it. I am magnificent
in God's eyes, yet I am removed from whom I thought I
was.
I see love, I feel love, and I touch love in all who come
into my world.
Yet in all this which is God, I am nothing. I am me.
I am a butterfly in motion.
I am free—
free from ego, free from pain, free from judgements of
how it should be.
I am free to be me.

Retreat

Retreat, retreat, retreat.
The soul is yearning for quietude, solitude, aloneness, a
     oneness with God.
Resting in the sacred house of love.
Providing a safe place to find stillness amidst the chaos
     of life.
My temple, the altar of all I believe, keeps my trembling
     heart grounded,
knowing that the temporary madness will cease when
     my soul,
my gracious heart can retreat.

Take Me

My beloved, I have surrendered completely into your
      divine will, and my heart is at the mercy of
      your request, knowing only that a life without
      unconditional love is no life at all.
So, take my hands and guide me.
Take my heart and love through me.
Take my soul so that you are the light that shines from
      within.
Take my arms so that those in need have a place to rest.
Take my breast so that the wounds of those are nurtured
      and healed.
Take my mind so that there is resolution to conflict.
Take my legs so that I may stand strong for those who
      are weak.
Take my feet so that I can walk with a gracious heart.
Loving you is loving me; knowing you is knowing me.
In this, I have eternal joy and everlasting peace.

Home

I have transcended my life of all I have known.
Every day is a metamorphosis.
Every breath I take is a miracle.
As I close my eyes, I see your beauty, your pure energy.
Everything dissolves away, and all that remains is light,
love, and absolute nothingness.
My restless heart has found peace;
I have come home to God.

Universal Key

Shanti, Shiva, Shakti, Maya.
With every breath of God and through the destruction of
    all that ever was,
Whatsoever you believe and the illusion of all there is . . .
only one truth remains.
When the walls have been knocked down,
the chains have been broken, and the door to your heart
    has been unlocked,
everything you are searching for is before you.
Go deeper within, and you will see the greatest love of
    all is God within you.
You have the universal key....
Ham Sa.

My Religion

As I awake to a new day,
I realize I have strayed. I'm lost between the physical
and the ethereal of my being.
My reasoning mind holds on to the logic of life,
yet my soul and my heart hold on to peace.
No suffering, no pain. . . .
I stand before myself on
either side of the two realities I create,
finding comfort in acceptance,
for this love that penetrates
every cell at the core of my being
cannot deny the God in everything I see,
every lesson, every moment of truth.
I am here, and you are here with me. . . .
The temple of God is home to my heart,
for every time I lose myself,
I call upon the illusion of all I believe.
I let go, free-fall, and finally I come home to me.
There is no excuse, no blame, and I have no regret.
There is no anger, no shame, and I cannot resent.
There is no sadness, no pain, for only love resides in my
       heart.
My religion is the happiness of me.

Seeker of Truth

I have only dreamt of a love so magnificent.
I have only prayed for a love so divine.
Here I am face to face with you.
My heart is full of love, and in this, I find suffering and
     pain.
Every cell of my body,
every fiber of my being wants to drown in the greatness
     of this love.
Let me swim; let me dive to new depths of loving you.
Let me be a channel of grace,
a seeker of truth.

Love Divine

You stand in the midst of love, and before you are a
    thousand faces of God.
All longing, all searching.
Can we, as humans, truly understand the depths of what
    we ask for?
Can we know what it would really feel like to be loved
    unconditionally?
Your soul craves for your physical being to embrace the
    truth of what you seek.
For a glimpse, you taste the essence of true love.
For a moment of bliss, you experience God's greatness.
Heaven's doors open to receive you,
then you realize the sacrifice to loving unconditionally is
    more painful than not.
God's love has claimed your existence;
you have been reborn into all you desire.
You have seen God through many eyes;
you have loved God through many hearts.
You have been intimate with God; you have connected to
    the souls of all you've touched.
In all your life experiences, the outer world you see is
    God loving you the way
you have always dreamed.
Your heart desires a true manifestation of lasting love.
To be loved unconditionally, you must embrace
    unconditional love and accept that within yourself.
In this, you will find the essence of all pain and suffering,
    the mirror of revelations.
The soul will know, and the heart will bleed—
free from all expectation—and only then will you have
    transcended the need for love,
and the manifestation of lasting love will have become
    divine.

Printed in the United States
152738LV00001B/55/P